FANTASTIC FAILS

Learning from Bad Ideas

GADGET DISASTERS

BY ELIZABETH PAGEL-HOGAN

CAPSTONE PRESS
a capstone imprint

Capstone Captivate is published by Capstone Press,
an imprint of Capstone.
1710 Roe Crest Drive
North Mankato, Minnesota 56003
www.capstonepub.com

Copyright © 2020 by Capstone. All rights reserved.
No part of this publication may be reproduced in whole or in part, or stored in a retrieval system, or transmitted in any form or by any means, electronic, mechanical, photocopying, recording, or otherwise, without written permission of the publisher.

Library of Congress Cataloging-in-Publication Data is available on the Library of Congress website.
ISBN: 978-1-5435-9211-5 (library binding)
ISBN: 978-1-4966-6620-8 (paperback)
ISBN: 978-1-5435-9215-3 (eBook PDF)

Summary: See some of the world's greatest gadget disasters from the palm of your hand. Find out how each gadget failed, what went wrong with its design or manufacture, and what programmers learned from their mistakes.

Image Credits
Alamy: Everett Collection, Inc., 37; Capstone Studio: Karon Dubke, 21, 22; Getty Images: AFP, 17, Ed Clark, 31, Popperfoto/Rolls Press, 18, SLADE Paul, 13, The Asahi Shimbun, 32, 33; Library of Congress: 5 (bottom); Newscom: CNP/Ron Sachs, 29, OUEST FRANCE/PHOTOPQR, 34, Polaris, 26; Science Source: Ton Kinsbergen, 9; Shutterstock: Akbaly, 45 (top), axeiz, 10, blambca, cover (illustration), bsd, 44 (bottom), DesignPrax, 44 (top), hanohiki, 41 (bottom), IMississHope, 45 (bottom), Leszek Kobusinski, 25, pio3, 42, Rigucci, cover (birds), Sergiy Kuzmin, 41 (top), Taweepat, cover (smoke); Wikimedia: Leonardo da Vinci National Museum of Science and Technology, 14, Mabalu, 6

Design Elements: Shutterstock

Editorial Credits
Editor: Mari Bolte; Designer: Jennifer Bergstrom; Media Researcher: Eric Gohl; Production Specialist: Laura Manthe

All internet sites appearing in back matter were available and accurate when this book was sent to press.

Printed and bound in the United States of America.
PA100

TABLE OF CONTENTS

CHAPTER

1 EERIE VOICES
EDISON'S TALKING DOLL 4

2 PLAYBACK PROBLEMS
THE LASERDISC 8

3 MOVIES IN THE DARK
POLAVISION 12

4 DISPOSABLE OUTFITS
PAPER CLOTHING 16

5 READING IT WRONG
READAMATIC ROBOT 20

6 WHEN YOUR PHONE BLOWS UP
SAMSUNG GALAXY NOTE 7 BATTERIES 24

7 BOOST ME UP
BELL ROCKET BELT 28

8 FLAILING FINGERS
RING 32

9 A REAL STINKER!
SMELL-O-VISION 36

10 OUT OF THE WAY!
SEGWAY 40

INVENTIONS BY KIDS 44
GLOSSARY 46
READ MORE 47
INTERNET SITES 47
INDEX 48

Words in **bold** are in the glossary.

PEOPLE HAVE ALWAYS WANTED TO SHOW OFF THE FASTEST, COOLEST, NEWEST GADGETS. Inventors are willing to try new ideas and materials to make those gadgets. But even the best planners have some ideas that turn out to be disasters. Learn how even great inventions turned out to be disasters.

CHAPTER 1
EERIE VOICES
EDISON'S TALKING DOLL

Thomas Edison was a busy inventor. One of his most popular inventions was the phonograph. The phonograph was a device that used a needle to pick up sounds from a spinning cylinder. Then it played the sounds through a loudspeaker. The first sound his phonograph played was the song "Mary Had a Little Lamb."

Edison dreamed of inventing a talking doll as early as 1877. That same year, he invented the phonograph. In 1890, he made the dolls a reality. He put a mini phonograph inside each doll. Children turned a key on the back of the doll and the doll "spoke" nursery rhymes.

HOW WE HEAR IT

1 A person speaks into the tube.

2 His or her voice causes a vibration. This pushes a needle back and forth in the pattern of the vibration, cutting grooves into a piece of metal foil.

3 The foil is wrapped around a cylinder, which is turned by a motor.

4 Another needle traces the grooves in the metal. Electrical impulses are created as the needle bounces along the grooves.

5 A horn converts the impulses into sound that can be heard.

How Many?

Thomas Edison filed 1,093 U.S. **patents** and held 2,332 total patents around the world. But Japanese inventor Shunpei Yamazaki has him beat. Yamazaki holds 16,836 active U.S. patents and has been named the inventor of more than 28,000 different patents. Yamazaki works in the fields of computer science and physics.

Thomas Edison (1847–1931)

FACT: After Edison's dolls failed, he started calling them "little monsters."

Edison's doll stood 22 inches (56 centimeters) tall and weighed 4 pounds (1.8 kilograms). The phonograph inside (right) was 7 inches (18 cm) tall.

At the time, a talking doll was astonishing. But the dolls were not very popular. They were expensive. Dolls with plain clothes cost $10. A doll with fancy clothes was $25, equal to about $530 in today's money.

The dolls said the same thing over and over. And they didn't sound nice. Even Edison described the voices as "exceedingly unpleasant."

The phonograph's cylinders were fragile and broke easily. This did not make them good toys for children.

Edison's Concre-ations

Inventors are willing to try making new products and using new materials, even if they seem strange or unusual. Thomas Edison had a factory that made concrete. His concrete was used to build Yankee Stadium for the New York Yankees baseball team. He had so much concrete he invented other ways to use it. He designed a case for his popular phonograph that was made of concrete. He created a working piano that had a concrete cabinet. He even had plans to build whole houses from concrete. But an invention isn't a success unless people like it and use it.

Edison made 10,000 dolls. But he sold fewer than 500. People didn't like the dolls and returned them. Records show that around 7,500 dolls were never moved from storage.

Lessons Learned

The technology wasn't right for talking toys during Edison's lifetime. Other talking toys came and went. After the invention of electronic microchips, though, talking toys became a hit.

CHAPTER 2
PLAYBACK PROBLEMS
THE LASERDISC

Sometimes even really great inventions are considered failures. They may get the job done, but if another similar invention does the job a little bit better, they fail. The LaserDisc is an example of this kind of invention.

David Paul Gregg invented the technology for LaserDiscs in 1958. He received a patent for it in 1961. A LaserDisc is a plastic disc about 12 inches (31 cm) wide. Lasers burn a sequence of holes into the disc to record sounds and images.

The LaserDisc solved some of the problems film **projectors** had. Film projectors were difficult to use. Rolls of film were large and heavy. Sometimes filmstrips tore or broke. The LaserDisc made it easier for people to watch movies and television shows at home. The invention also made it easier for schools to show films.

To watch movies at home or at school, people needed a special LaserDisc player. A laser in the player read the code and transformed the information into sounds and images.

The Philips company released LaserDiscs to the public in 1978. They worked great. The quality of the images and sounds was good.

Jaws was the first movie recorded onto a LaserDisc.

But there were a few problems. The LaserDiscs were large. Each disc weighed about half a pound (227 grams). They were also fragile. Their short running time was another problem. Only an hour of video could be played on each side. And LaserDisc players were very expensive.

Finally, a new technology had arrived a year before LaserDiscs became available. The videocassette was a rectangular plastic case with a videotape inside.

Videocassettes stored media on magnetic tape.

Videocassettes could hold several hours of video. The picture was not as high quality as one from a LaserDisc. But they were cheaper. LaserDiscs cost five times more to make.

FACT: Weighing in at half a pound and stretching 12 inches (31 centimeters) wide, LaserDiscs were quite large. To compare, CDs and DVDs weigh half an ounce (14 grams) and are 4.7 inches (12 cm) wide.

And videocassettes could do something LaserDiscs couldn't do—they were recordable. People could record shows from their home televisions onto the videocassettes. People could even watch one show on one channel and record onto a videocassette from a different channel.

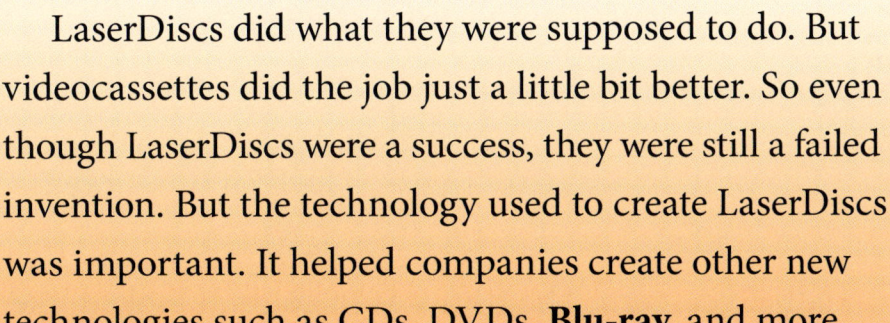

Lessons Learned

LaserDiscs did what they were supposed to do. But videocassettes did the job just a little bit better. So even though LaserDiscs were a success, they were still a failed invention. But the technology used to create LaserDiscs was important. It helped companies create other new technologies such as CDs, DVDs, **Blu-ray**, and more.

11

Chapter 3
Movies in the Dark
Polavision

Inventors often know what people want, but don't have the technology to create a product that people love.

People in the mid- to late 1900s loved their Polaroid cameras. With other cameras, people had to take their film to a developer and wait several days for their photographs. But Polaroid cameras developed their photographs instantly.

People also loved taking home movies. In the 1970s, people recorded films and home movies with sound on Super 8 film. But like regular camera film, Super 8 film still had to be developed.

What if people could make movies at home that could be developed instantly? In 1977, Polaroid introduced Polavision.

The product was easy to use. The film was stored in a **cartridge**. The cartridge was easy to load into the handheld camera. The film was in color. It looked like a great product.

FACT: The first Polaroid camera was sold in 1948 for $89.95. By 1956, more than 1 million had been sold. The first color Polaroid film was created in 1963.

Inventor Edwin Land shows off the Polavision in 1977.

The Polavision Viewer had a 12-inch (31-cm) screen. The colors in the picture were so dense that the home movies could not be projected onto a larger screen.

But there were big problems. The film could only record for two and a half minutes, and there was no sound. If people filmed in low light, the images weren't clear. And a special Polavision player was needed to see their short, silent, and possibly dark home movies.

Polaroid only sold Polavision cameras and projectors for two years. The company lost a lot of money on this gadget disaster.

FACT: The cartridge was a self-contained film processing center. A pod of developing liquid was inside. Placing the cartridge in the viewer started the processing. It took about a minute to complete.

The First Home Videos

The first video recording technology was invented in the 1920s. The first videotape recorder (VTR) was sold in 1956. It cost $50,000. The first videocassette recorder (VCR) for home use was sold in 1971.

By the 1980s, both Polavision and Super 8 films had faded from the market. Videocassettes and handheld video cameras made it easy to take home movies and watch them at home.

Lessons Learned

The idea of instant home movies people could watch right away was a good one. But the technology just wasn't there to make a product that worked well. Longer videos, easier ways to watch them, better picture quality, and sound would have made a big difference.

Chapter 4
Disposable Outfits
Paper Clothing

Some inventors take two things that have been around for a long time and blend them together to create a new and exciting idea. This idea can transform people lives, or it can be a total flop. Some ideas are in the middle.

People have worn clothing for thousands of years. And people have used paper for centuries. So why not use paper clothing?

This was a real invention that became a hit in the 1960s. By 1967, people could buy paper clothing in top department stores. Clothing companies made all kinds of paper clothes. Men had paper vests. Women wore paper bridal gowns. Children even had paper clothes. There were paper swimsuits, although they only lasted one or two wears.

Paper clothes were inexpensive and very interesting. Many had eye-catching, artistic designs. Some even had patterns that buyers could color in on their own. Fashion designers turned it into high-end **couture**.

Party Time

Paper clothing was first created for hospital use. It was hygienic and could be thrown away after being used. Later, paper companies made paper dresses to match the party supplies they were selling, such as paper cups, tablecloths, and napkins. The pattern of the dresses matched the pattern on the paper tableware. Sometimes the dresses would come with coupons for other paper products.

Fashion models in Paris showed off a line of paper outfits in 1967.

Paper clothes were made from a disposable material that was slightly fire- and water-resistant. It is similar to disposable bibs used in dentists' offices.

Clothing made from paper was considered a novelty. Hotels would stock paper clothing in their gift shops. Guests could buy clothes on vacation and then throw them away before they left.

Paper clothes didn't last as long as real clothing or as a fashion trend. They weren't very comfortable. They didn't fit very well. Sometimes the colors wore off. They were also **flammable**. Although outfits could be refreshed by a quick iron, the heat from the iron often removed any protection against water or fire originally added to the material. People worried about wearing clothing that could easily catch fire.

People wore them once or twice, then threw the clothes away. The disposable nature made people believe they weren't worth the money. Paper clothing disappeared from clothing stores by 1968.

Lessons Learned

Some inventions are only popular for a short time. These ideas are trends. They show inventors that people are willing to experiment and try new things. But if an idea isn't practical, it won't last.

Invented Before Its Time

Sometimes an inventor has a great idea but it takes a while to catch on. In 1902, Mary Anderson rode a streetcar in New York City. She noticed that the driver had to keep getting out to wipe snow off the streetcar's window. She wondered if there was a way for snow to be removed without stopping the car. So she developed hand-operated windshield wipers. When she tried to sell her invention to car companies, they were not interested. But after 1920, more and more people owned cars, and the car companies finally recognized the value of windshield wipers.

CHAPTER 5
READING IT WRONG
READAMATIC ROBOT

Many inventions are meant to solve problems that people face. But sometimes inventions cause more problems than they solve. The Readamatic Robot was the perfect example of an unhelpful invention.

The Readamatic Robot was invented in 1963. It was a device made of a small box and metal arm with a second metal bar at one end. The metal arm stretched over the page in a book. The metal bar sat on a page under the words. As a person read, the Readamatic Robot arm moved down the page.

One goal of the Readamatic Robot was to help people read faster. The second goal was to help struggling readers slow down and understand more of what they read.

The Readamatic Robot could be adjusted to fit different kinds of books with different amounts of words per page. By turning a knob on the box, readers could change the speed of the metal bar. They could speed it up or slow it down.

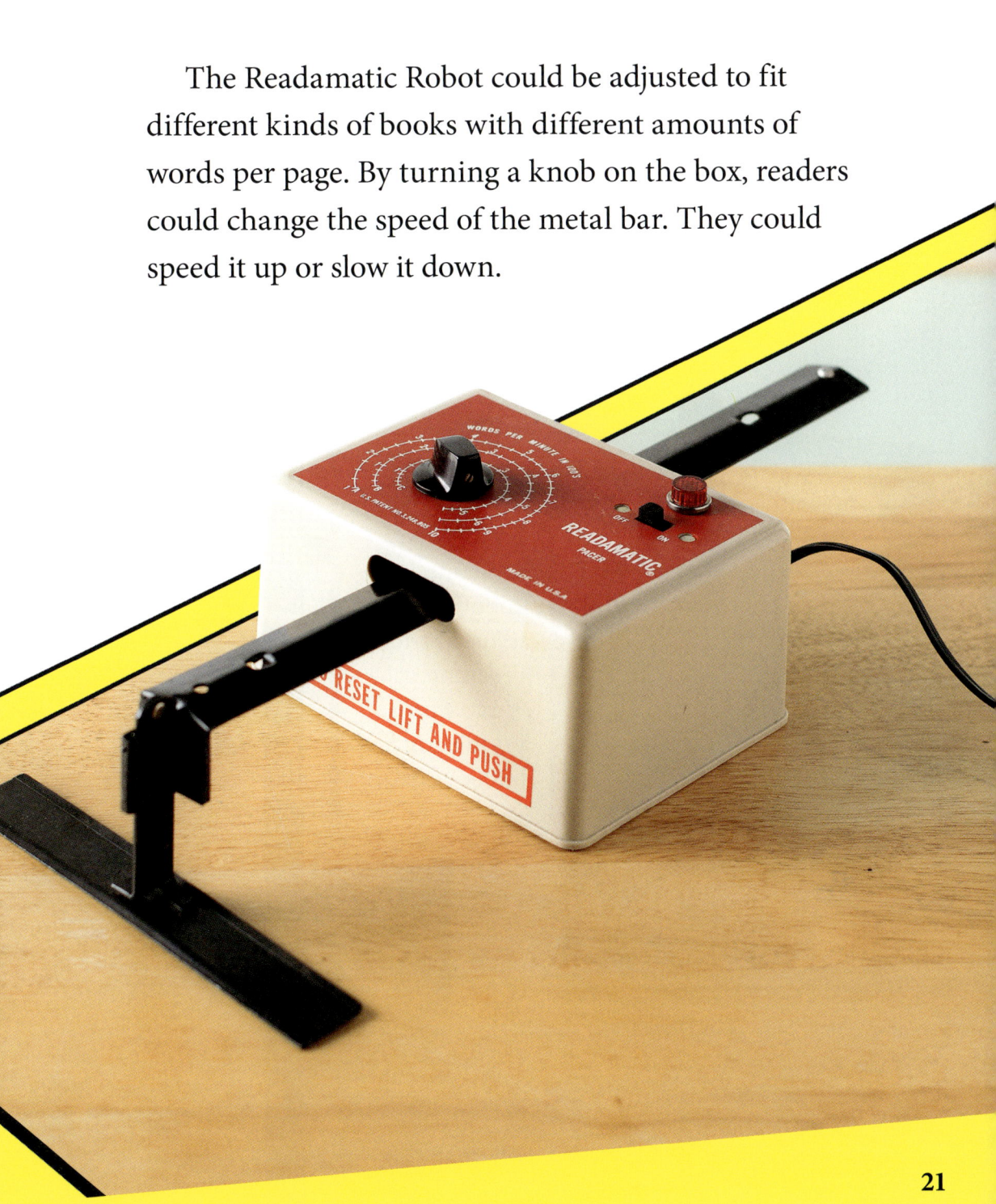

Although the idea of a robot to help people read better was a good one, the Readamatic Robot was a bad gadget.

> **FACT:** Sometimes inventions are just silly. In 2015, an inventor in Japan created the Tomatan. It is a robot that feeds people tomatoes while they run. It weighs 17.5 pounds (7.7 kilograms) and holds six tomatoes at a time.

The Readamatic Robot could be adjusted from a reading pace of 100 words a minute to 1,000.

The sound of the metal bar scratching on the page was distracting. The whirring of the motor was distracting too. The long metal arm blocked part of the page. In the end, the same result could be created by readers holding a ruler under the lines as they read.

Lessons Learned

Sometimes things designed to help actually create more of a problem. Instead of helping people to read, the Readamatic Robot made it harder for them to concentrate.

Helpful Robots

Some robots are very helpful. The first robot vacuum came out in 1996. Now they are popular. They use a variety of **sensors** to move around homes and clean up dirt. Some have special brushes or use **ultraviolet** (UV) technology to kill germs. Some are specially designed to clean carpets or mop hard flooring.

CHAPTER 6
WHEN YOUR PHONE BLOWS UP

SAMSUNG GALAXY NOTE 7 BATTERIES

Most of the time, a gadget disaster just means a new idea doesn't work. But some gadget disasters can cause serious damage and even put people in danger.

In August 2016, Samsung launched a new model of a smartphone called the Note 7. The phone had received great advance reviews. Preorders were at a record high. Samsung forecasted it would ship 15 million phones around the world before the end of the year.

Soon after people started using the new phones, though, they noticed there was a huge problem. Some of the phones unexpectedly exploded and burst into flames. People were injured by the fires. One fire destroyed a person's vehicle. Another fire caused the evacuation of an airplane. Eventually, the phone was banned on all flights.

The company acted quickly. Fourteen days after its launch, sales were suspended. A **recall** was sent out. Replacement phones were sent out by the end of September. But then the replacement phones also started catching fire!

Cell phone batteries are designed to store as much energy as they can. If that energy is suddenly released, phones can melt and fires can start.

Investigators learned that the batteries in the phones caused the explosions and fires. Samsung purchased the batteries from two different **manufacturers**. The two different kinds of batteries had two different problems.

In one battery, the positive and negative **electrodes** touched and caused a **short circuit**. The other battery had a sharp edge inside. That edge pierced the battery's insulation and caused a short circuit. The short circuits were what caused the fires.

Samsung ended up sending out an update that would **brick** all Note 7s. They asked Note 7 customers to return their phones. In the end, the loss of presales, profits, and future sales hurt the company. The Note 7 cost Samsung $17 billion.

Lessons Learned

Samsung acted quickly to contact customers and recall the dangerous batteries. But if they hadn't acted so quickly to release the phone in the first place, engineers would have had more time to discover potential problems. The promise of a smaller phone with a larger battery wasn't something that could be delivered quickly.

Samsung shared information with other manufacturers to help prevent these kinds of problems in future technology. Manufacturers also agreed to do even more testing on technology to ensure its safety before selling to consumers.

CHAPTER 7
BOOST ME UP
BELL ROCKET BELT

In the 1950s, Wendell Moore had an idea. He decided the world needed a rocket booster pack to help people leap long distances. As an employee at Bell Aerosystems, a huge **aviation** company, he had the skills and resources to make that possible.

The first Bell Rocket Belt looked like a large backpack with handles. It had a fuel tank and two nozzles. The fuel tank held 5 gallons (19 liters) of concentrated hydrogen peroxide. When the pilot pressed the controls, fuel was forced out of the tanks. The fuel reacted with silver plates, which turned it into highly pressurized steam. The steam exited through the nozzles and lifted the pilot into the air.

In early test flights, the pilot and rocket booster pack often wobbled and went off balance. The pilot and rocket belt were attached to a safety tether so they would not fly too high.

The Bell Rocket Belt weighs 65 pounds (30 kg).

Moore was one of the test pilots. During one demonstration, his pack tilted and broke the tether. Moore fell from the air. He broke his kneecap. After that, Moore didn't make any more test flights. But he didn't stop working on the Rocket Belt.

The new test pilot, Harold Graham, practiced over and over. He could launch 4 feet (1.2 meters) in the air and zoom about 100 feet (31 m) forward before landing. The first flight lasted 13 seconds. Eventually, he learned how to fly in a circle, soar over cars, and slip between trees. But the belt itself didn't improve much. Its flight time maxed out at 21 seconds.

The U.S. Army wanted to see the belt in 1961. But officials weren't impressed. The flight time was too short. Inventors worked on a new version that used superheated water vapor for fuel.

Successful Squirt Guns

Another inventor who didn't give up after one try was Lonnie Johnson. In 1986, Lonnie received a patent for a device he called the "Power Drencher." It combined a water bottle with a squirt gun. It used air pressure to shoot water farther than a regular squirt gun. Eventually, it was renamed the Super Soaker and has been a huge success.

That didn't help. The fuel was so hot that pilots had to wear insulating clothes to protect themselves from burns. In addition, the height the belt flew at was too low for a parachute to work. If the engine failed in the sky, the pilot would likely be injured.

Harold Graham shows off the Bell Rocket Belt in 1961.

Lessons Learned

Even though the Bell Rocket Belt didn't take off like Moore hoped, it is still being used, mostly for entertainment. It has been used during events at Disneyland, in the opening ceremonies for the 1984 and 1996 Summer Olympics, and in a James Bond movie.

CHAPTER 8
FLAILING FINGERS RING

Wearable technology sounds really exciting. Some people wear headphones in their ears or smart watches on their wrists. The company Logbar promised people they could have the power of technology at their fingertips—literally! Logbar's product, a large silver ring, would connect with a smartphone. The wearer could get alerts, send texts, change his or her phone's volume, turn on lights, or even pay bills with gestures.

In 2014, the still-small company raised money through **crowdfunding**. Its goal was $250,000. More than 5,000 people contributed. The campaign raised $880,000 in 36 days.

Ring wearers could trace letters in the air with their fingers. The letters would be translated into texts.

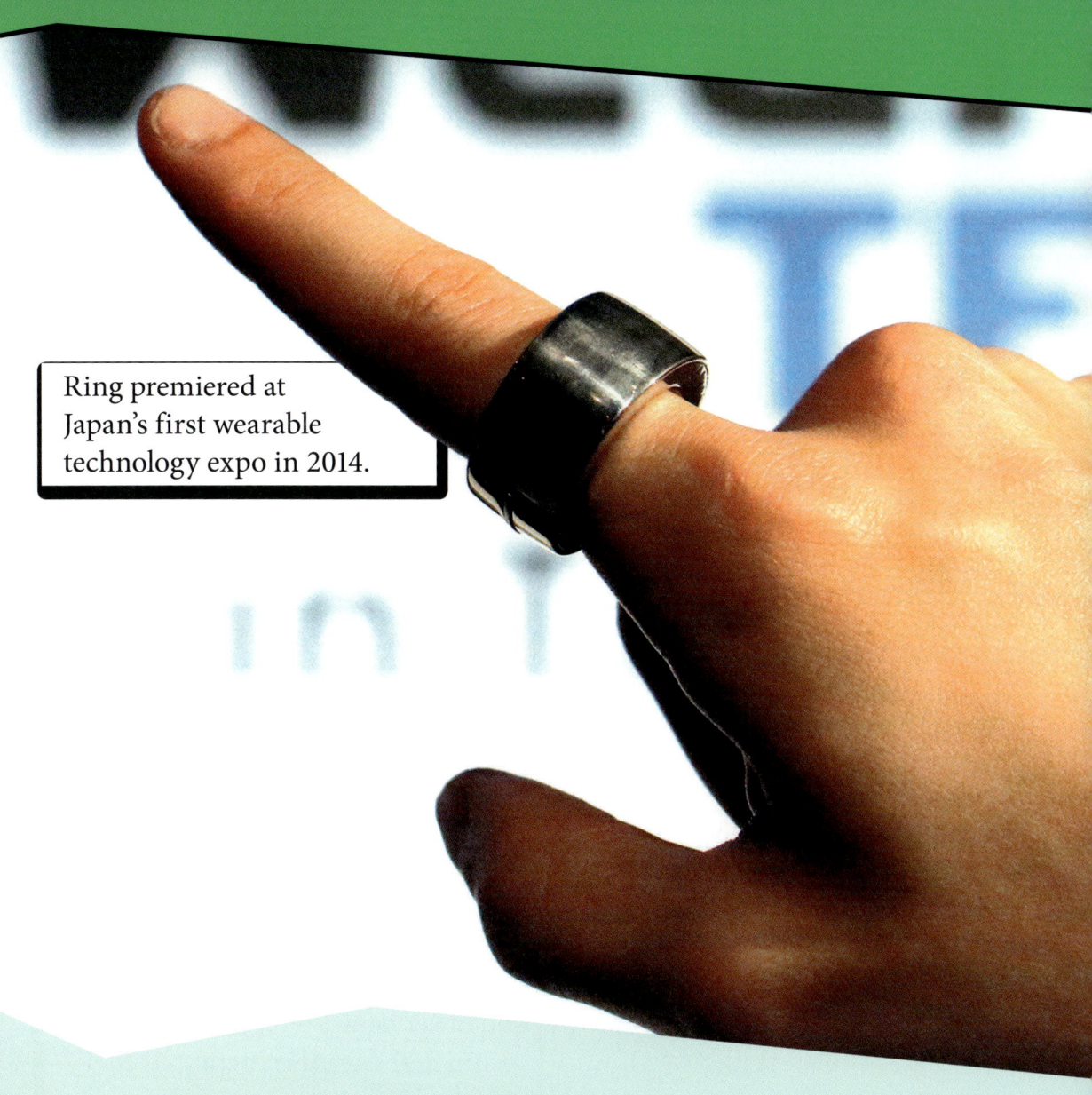

Ring premiered at Japan's first wearable technology expo in 2014.

Wash Your Hands!

Sometimes the simplest solution isn't a new invention. Inventor Philipp Zumtobel didn't like the smudges on his phone screen, so he invented Phone Fingers. But these little rubber finger covers were too hard to put on and take off. The simplest solution to dirty phone screens was to only use the phone with clean hands.

When people got their Ring, they were disappointed. Many people felt it was too thick to wear comfortably on a finger. It also only came in three sizes, which limited who could use it. When users tried gesturing, most of the time nothing happened.

Smart Eyewear

Many inventors and companies are working on new kinds of wearable tech. Google introduced Google Glass. Google Glass is wearable smart technology that looks like glasses.

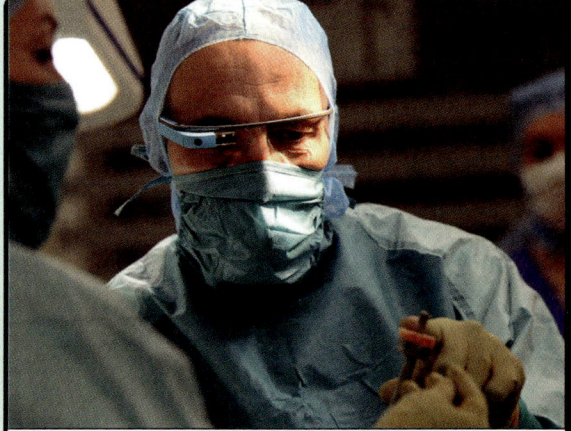

Doctors have used Google Glass and other smart technology to record and store the operations they perform. Others have used them to livestream procedures to medical schools around the world.

People had concerns. Some worried the device would invade their privacy if users recorded conversations without permission. Businesses were worried Google Glass might help users break the law, such as by recording movies in theaters. But doctors, journalists, and people with autism and vision problems have benefited from Google Glass.

In order to activate Ring, users pressed a small button on the side of the device. A small LED light flashed to show that Ring was ready. But the light didn't always work. Other people reported that it refused to pair with their other smart technology.

People learned that the app always had to be open on their smartphones for an action to work. In order to control household appliances, people had to buy another device called the Ring Hub.

Instead of turning on a phone, connecting Ring, and trying a gesture that might not do anything, it was easier for people to just use their smartphones by themselves.

Lessons Learned

The idea for Ring was a good one. But the execution was a fail. It was too bulky and too inconvenient to use. The technology didn't work all the time, and it wasn't as futuristic as promised. But that didn't stop other inventors. Today there are smart rings that track your activity levels, heart rate, and body temperature. Others allow you to pay for things, lock your car, and get access to your online accounts.

CHAPTER 9
A REAL STINKER!
SMELL-O-VISION

The first movies were a treat for the eyes, and later, the ears. Why not the nose too?

In the 1920s and 1930s, some theater owners experimented with blowing smells into theaters while people watched movies. In big theaters, not everyone smelled the odors. Sometimes the scents mixed and did not smell good. Those smells lingered for a long time.

Inventor Hans Laube had a new plan. His invention would send scents to each individual seat in the theater. He shared his first idea for "Scentovision" at the 1939 New York World's Fair. No one was interested.

Laube didn't get discouraged. In 1954, he filed for a patent for Smell-O-Vision. Smell-O-Vision was controlled by the "smell brain." The smell brain was a circular belt with little perfume capsules. As the movie played, the smell brain rotated under the seats. At certain points during the movie, a needle pierced the capsules. Fans blew the scents up to the viewer.

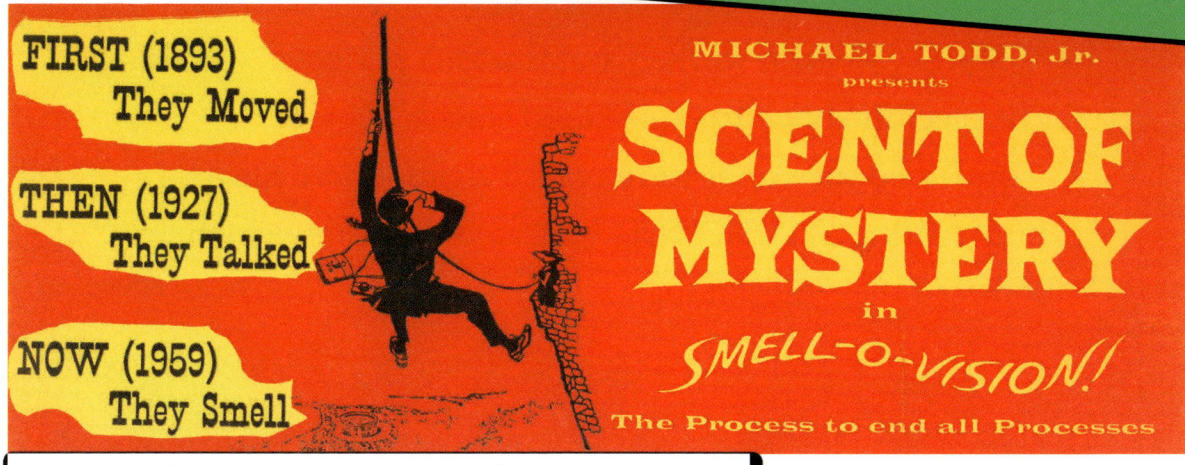

Scent of Mystery was later released—without smells—under the name *Holiday in Spain*.

In the late 1960s, Laube met movie producer Mike Todd Jr. Todd helped make the first movie to use Smell-O-Vision, *Scent of Mystery*. There was a peach smell for the scene in the peach orchard. There was a grape aroma for the scene when a wine barrel fell off a cart. When one character was onscreen, viewers smelled tobacco.

Smelly Competition

At the same time Smell-O-Vision launched, another company offered movie smells. AromaRama blew scents through the theater's air conditioning system. It included 72 smells to pair with the movie *Behind the Great Wall*. People called this competition between the two movies the battle of the "smellies."

Smell-O-Vision worked, but it wasn't perfect. The machine hissed as it released smells. People complained the scents didn't reach them. There was loud sniffing as viewers tried to catch the scent, which bothered their neighbors.

TIMELINE OF ON-SCREEN SUCCESSES

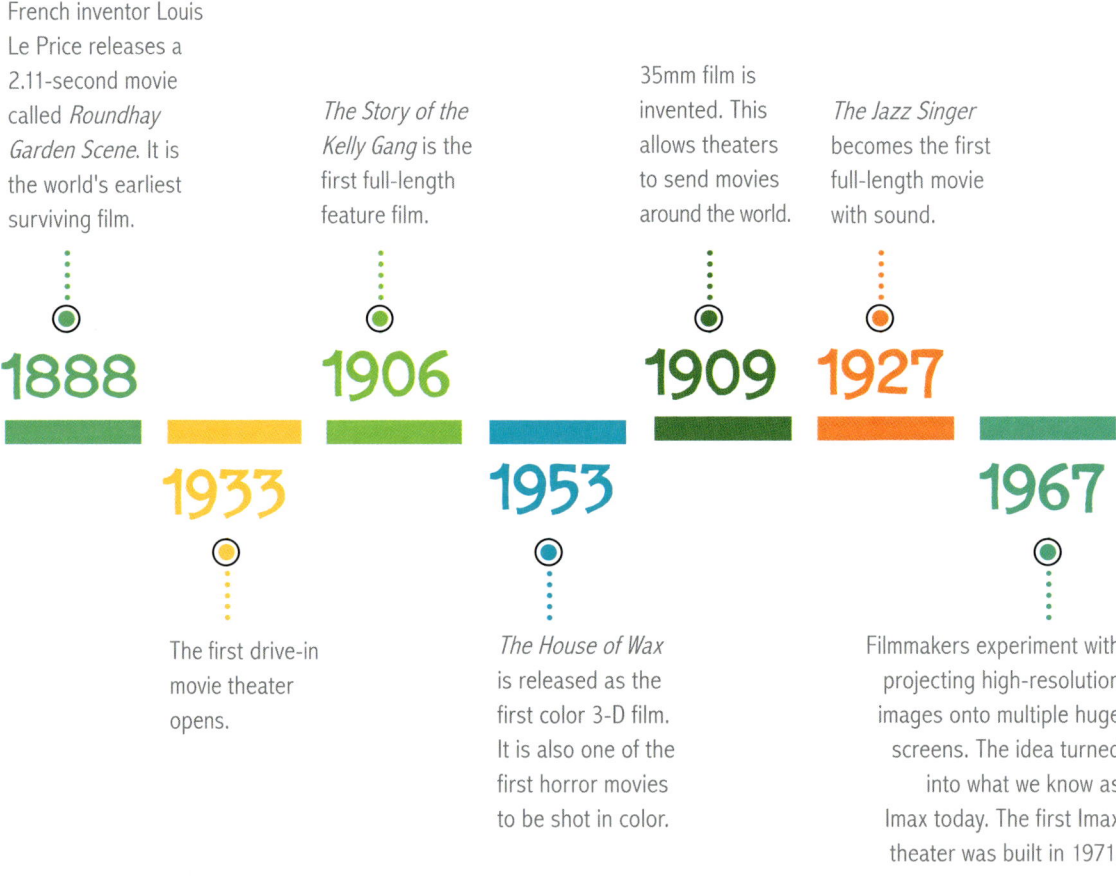

French inventor Louis Le Price releases a 2.11-second movie called *Roundhay Garden Scene*. It is the world's earliest surviving film.

1888

The Story of the Kelly Gang is the first full-length feature film.

1906

35mm film is invented. This allows theaters to send movies around the world.

1909

The Jazz Singer becomes the first full-length movie with sound.

1927

1933

The first drive-in movie theater opens.

1953

The House of Wax is released as the first color 3-D film. It is also one of the first horror movies to be shot in color.

1967

Filmmakers experiment with projecting high-resolution images onto multiple huge screens. The idea turned into what we know as Imax today. The first Imax theater was built in 1971.

Even when technical problems with the smell brain were fixed, too many people had complaints. To add insult to injury, the movie didn't get good reviews.

Lessons Learned

Smell-O-Vision was set up in only three theaters, and it was such a failure that no other theaters wanted to try. The creators tried to improve the movie's problems, but by then word had spread. Audiences couldn't be bothered to see *Scent of Mystery*.

Inventors have not given up on mixing movies and smells, though. Some movie creators produced scratch-and-sniff cards that people scratched during the movie. Others created devices that attach to computers and release smells when people visit certain websites. This idea may be waiting for the right inventor.

Chapter 10
Out of the Way!

Segway

Some gadgets work great. They do just what the inventor hoped. But if there's not a market for them, they won't sell.

The Segway is an electric vehicle. It has two wheels, a platform, and a handlebar. A person rides a Segway by standing on the platform and holding on to the handles. With the smallest of motions, the Segway moves forward or backward.

Inventor Dean Kamen launched the Segway in 2001. At first, people were excited about this new way to get around. The Segway worked just as the developers said it would.

It was hoped that the Segway would become a new mode of transportation. Ads claimed it would become a part of everyday life, just like cell phones and the internet.

SEGWAY PARTS

handlebar
riders hold the handlebar when the Segway is in motion

steerable frame
controls the Segway; the rider leans the frame to turn

height adjustment knob
adjusts the handlebar height

mats
protect the sensors underneath; provide a comfortable standing surface for the rider

indicator lights
indicate whether the Segway is ready to ride; show battery power

fenders
keep rocks, sand, and mud from flying up in the air

power base and batteries
Segways have two batteries; they need to be charged after 12 hours of use.

wheels
how the Segway moves

41

There were some drawbacks to the wonder machine. It came with a $5,000 to $6,000 price tag, which was as much as a used car.

Another issue was that the Segway was a unique-looking vehicle. Riders thought they might look silly riding one. Helmets and safety pads were recommended accessories. If it rained or snowed, there was no way to escape getting wet. You could easily hop off a scooter or skateboard and go inside in bad weather. But it's harder to move a 100-pound (45-kilogram) Segway.

FACT: Segway inventor Dean Kamen had other successes. The AutoSyringe helped people with diabetes get insulin. In 2005, he was inducted into the National Inventors Hall of Fame.

Segways are 11 times more efficient than the average car.

People had other questions too. Where would you park it? Where would you charge the battery? Where could you ride one? Its top speed was 12.5 miles (20 kilometers) per hour—too slow for the road, but too fast for the sidewalk. Some cities ended up banning Segways on both.

In the end, the biggest problem was that people didn't really need a Segway. It was a novelty, but not something they wanted to use on a regular basis.

Lessons Learned

Even though the Segway works well, it did not change the way people live or work on a daily basis. And owning one could be a challenge. Some places considered them to be motor vehicles and required them to be registered and insured. Some places required the rider to be licensed. Some didn't allow riders to carry any packages or baggage while riding. Police officers didn't know whether they should tell riders to get on or off the sidewalk. It is a successful invention but a failed innovation.

INVENTIONS BY KIDS

Not all inventors are adults. Kids invent things that have made life easier, more fun, and less challenging.

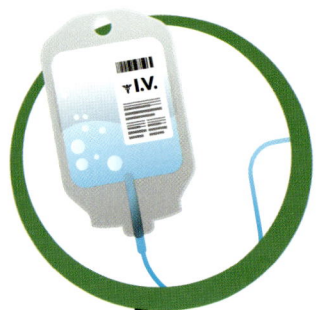

Kylie Simonds was 8 years old when she was diagnosed with cancer. While she received chemotherapy, she had to push a heavy IV pole around. The wires were easy to trip over. Kylie invented a portable IV backpack in 2014. She is still working on making it available to the public.

Suman Mulumudi was in high school when he designed an iPhone case for people with medical conditions. It turns smartphones into stethoscopes using the phone's microphone. Patients can check their heart health and send information to their doctors.

In 2012, **Catherine Wong**, 17, came up with a way to help doctors see patients' heartbeats on a smartphone screen. Usually, a person's heartbeat is monitored with an electrocardiogram (EKG) machine. But they are usually only found at a doctor's office or a hospital. Catherine's invention would make it possible for anyone to gather that data anywhere, at any time. This is especially helpful in parts of the world where there are no hospitals.

In 1930, 16-year-old **George Nissen** first saw trapeze artists fall safely into a net. The net stretched and bounced the artists high into the air. Nissen wondered if he could make something that would let a person bounce longer. He built a prototype trampoline in 1937. Today trampolines are available to everyone.

Frank Epperson was 11 when he forgot his soft drink outside in the cold. He had left a stirring stick in the glass. When he discovered it in the morning, he saw it was frozen solid but fun to lick. Epperson patented the popsicle in 1924.

In 1850, 12-year-old **Margaret E. Knight** was working at a cotton mill when she saw a young boy killed by machinery. She invented a safety mechanism that was soon installed in every mill. Her invention saved lives.

In 1999, **Cassidy Goldstein** realized she could keep using worn-down crayons by holding them in small tubes that are used to keep flower stems fresh. Her invention helped reduce crayon waste. In 2006, she won the Youth Inventor of the Year award.

GLOSSARY

aviation (AY-vee-ay-shun)—the industry that builds airplanes

Blu-ray (BLOO-RAY)—a digital storage format that uses compact discs

brick (BRIK)—to make a smartphone or other electronic device completely, and usually permanently, unusable

cartridge (KAHR-trij)—a container holding a spool of photographic film

couture (koo-TOO-uhr)—fashionable clothes that are made to measure to a person's specific size and style requirements

crowdfunding (KROWD-fuhn-dingh)—funding a project or business by raising small amounts of money from many people, usually over the internet

electrode (e-LEK-trode)—a point where an electric current can flow into or out of

flammable (FLA-muh-buhl)—likely to catch fire

manufacturer (man-yuh-FAK-chur-ur)—a person or company that makes products

patent (PAT-uhnt)—a legal document giving someone sole rights to make or sell a product

projector (pruh-JEK-tuhr)—a device used to project an image onto a large surface, such as a screen or wall

recall (RE-kahl)—an official order to return a faulty product

sensor (SEN-sor)—a device that detects change, such as heat, light, sound, or motion

short circuit (SHORT SUR-kuht)—a connection of lower resistance that is accidentally made between points on a circuit where the resistance is usually much greater; short circuits can occur when electrical wires or connections are damaged

ultraviolet (uhl-truh-VYE-uh-lit)—rays of light that cannot be seen by the human eye

READ MORE

Boyer, Crispin. *Famous Fails!: Mighty Mistakes, Mega Mishaps & How a Mess Can Lead to Success!* Washington, D.C.: National Geographic, 2016.

Reynolds, Luke. *Fantastic Failures: True Stories of People Who Changed the World by Falling Down First.* New York: Aladdin, 2018.

Rhatigan, Joe. *Wacky Inventions of the Future: Weird Inventions that Seem Too Crazy to Be Real!* Lake Forest, CA: Walter Foster Jr., 2019.

INTERNET SITES

National Inventors Hall of Fame
https://www.invent.org

Kid Inventor's Day
http://www.kidinventorsday.com/contests.htm

The Tech Interactive
https://www.thetech.org

INDEX

Anderson, Mary, 19
AromaRama, 37
AutoSyringe, 42

Bell Aerosystems, 28
Bell Rocket Belt, 28–31

Edison's Talking Doll, 4–7
Edison, Thomas, 4, 5, 6, 7

film projectors, 8, 14

Google Glass, 34
Graham, Harold, 30, 31
Gregg, David Paul, 8

Johnson, Lonnie, 30

Kamen, Dean, 40, 42

Land, Edwin, 13
LaserDiscs, 8–11
Laube, Hans, 36, 37

microchips, 7
Moore, Wendell, 28, 29, 31

Paper Clothing, 16–19
patents, 5, 6, 20, 30
phonographs, 4, 5, 6
Polaroid cameras, 12, 13
Polavision, 12–15

Readamatic Robot, 20–23
recalls, 25, 27
recording equipment, 11, 12, 15
Ring, 32–35
robot vacuums, 23

Samsung Galaxy Note 7 Batteries, 24–27
Scent of Mystery, 37
Segways, 40–43
Smell-O-Vision, 36–39
Super 8 film, 12, 15
Super Soakers, 30

Todd Jr., Mike, 37
Tomatan, 22

videocassettes, 10, 11, 15

Yamazaki, Shunpei, 5

Zumtobel, Philipp, 33